Honorifics

Honorifics
Cynthia Miller

Nine
Arches
Press

Honorifics
Cynthia Miller

ISBN: 978-1-913437-15-2
eISBN: 978-1-913437-16-9

Cover artwork: © Gordon Cheung, 'Jan Davidsz. De Heem I (Small New Order) 2015'. www.gordoncheung.com

First published June 2021 by:

Nine Arches Press
Unit 14, Sir Frank Whittle Business Centre,
Great Central Way, Rugby.
CV21 3XH
United Kingdom

www.ninearchespress.com

Nine Arches Press is supported using public funding by Arts Council England.

Supported using public funding by
ARTS COUNCIL
ENGLAND

CONTENTS

Sayang / Sayang

n. / love
I have lived with this word
for 28 years and only now
is it taking root in my mouth.   See also: beloved, sweetheart

n. / waste
The thought of throwing food away.
The last bite of beef noodles,
gone rubbery and cold. Go on,
don't make me save it.   See also: regretful loss

n. / pity
All this fruit left on the branch,
steeping in its own rot.
Who knows how long we have
before a plastic bag
of windfall rambutans
turns into sweet slop.   See also:
We'll eat it anyway / yes darling /
my dearest / love is always dear
/ love / is never a waste / love is
eating scraps for fear of waste / love
is / chiding you to finish your plate /
love, eat up / eat up love / what a
pity / such a shame to waste love /
love, how much we've wasted

Portmeirion

"[English] has no grammar to describe something which
has already happened for you and which will be for me."
  – Carlo Rovelli

1.

Physicists debate
    whether when we
remember something
    we access
that original memory
    or a shortcut in the brain.

There is debate, too,
    amongst scientists
over whether too many
    shortcuts might,
over time, disintegrate
    the source memory.

The way English teachers
    year after year
kept photocopying
    the photocopies
until the original text
    faded completely.

The way oil
    from fingertips
can destroy
    a precious document
over time
    if handled too often.

The way I keep
   memories in
a temperature-controlled
   vault and hide the key
at the back of the
   cupboard of my mind.

NASA recently photographed
   a far-off star
orbiting a far-off
   planet, light years
from us, already winked
   out of our future.

2.

Last Christmas
   my mother gave me
a Portmeirion cup,
   last one from her beloved
wedding set, a wreath of
   dark leaves on its lip.

She had wrapped it
   in soft cotton t-shirts
and blue bubble wrap,
   gently tucked it in her
carry-on, a small bird
   travelling miles to reach me.

One day I saw a similar set
   in a charity shop,
dinner plate bloom of
   forget-me-nots and
heartsease, and felt a black hole
   yawn open inside me.

Though it has yet to come,
   it's coming.
Though it has yet to happen,
   it's happening.
This is the only way to explain
   how afraid I am of my mother dying:

My fear is a collapsing star
   eating all light.
The cup is still in the
   cupboard, untouched.

3.

(When the old family photos came into my possession, I looked at them so regularly I gradually convinced myself that I remembered specific events – my 3rd birthday, Chinese New Year '98 – though of course I didn't. The mind loves tricking itself.)

(The rest of the wedding china is kept in a storage box, perfect and unused. By which I mean safe. Not from chipping or breakages, safe, by which I mean safe from me.)

(There is no good reason at present for this anticipatory grief. I am inside its dark whale belly. I am waiting to be let loose. I am waiting to be vomited up. I have lost track of which one of us is the ghost and which is the haunted thing. The garden inside the vaulted cupboard of my mind is in full, glorious, out-of-season bloom: ceramic rhododendrons, dog rose, lilacs, butterflies and a Bee, my mother's mother, humming like a gentle oracle.)

4.

The photocopied page has no resemblance to the original textbook. No one even knows if the book still exists or indeed if it ever existed. When I go to check it out, the library has never heard of it. The handout is a blurry photo of a jadeite cup and saucer, or it is a poem in the shape of the Hanging Gardens of Babylon, or it is a feeling of a plug socket being improperly grounded, as told from the perspective of electricity. A crackling charge lingers. I look at the page. In the top left corner is a puckered shadow of an old staple copied again and again over the years. Ghost trapped in an AP English worksheet. That old familiar feeling, like someone has reached back in time and dragged me out of cold storage.

5.

The first circle
>   is a litany of laurel leaves around the edge.

The second circle
>   is the one I pace into the ground.

The third circle
>   is a dropped headlamp, looping small moons.

My body takes on sadness the way lily pollen stains everything.
>   Accidentally, gently, permanently.

Summer preserves haibun

after Aimee Nezhukumatathil

Thinking about pickling dark strips of stars and preserving them in vinegar. By the end of the day, every point of light small as a pink peppercorn, ready to be scooped out with fingers and eaten whole. By the end of the week, a galaxy of jars lighting up my pantry, each hand-labelled: *first night in Crete; full moon marmalade; Chania harbour w/ Venus in distance, best before December.* The kitchen humming like a Geiger counter, piccalilli ticking. I swam for miles that summer. Relished the sour pull of my shoulders as I carved through saltwater with just my arms, rarely kicking, preserving my energy for the way back.

after the storm

the ferry was cleared for travel

carrying long-life goods

& a memory of heat

for winter

Self-portrait as things that let the light in

skylight
(I winch myself open daily)

air well in a Peranakan townhouse
(imagine a courtyard holding onto daylight and rain long after it
passes, a study in the architecture of the sublime)

capiz
(there is a church in the Philippines with windows made only of
squares of this shell, light so thick it is a congregation streaming
in and filling every pew, you could lean your whole body weight
against it, press your hand to the oyster tongue pulse of it)

Proxima b

"[This] is the most astounding conclusion arrived
at in the whole of contemporary physics."
 – Carlo Rovelli

Say, for the purposes of this example, I'm on Proxima Centauri b
and you're on Earth. I'm lying on my front in the sleeping pod with
a satellite phone tucked under my chin, kicking my legs, asking you
what you're doing right now. The "now" is important; I'll return to
this later. I can hear the familiar clatter of you moving around the
small kitchen, opening drawers, munching on sweet chilli crisps as
you peek at dinner in the oven. My longing telescopes. I pretend
I'm right there with you.

o

According to physics, there is no universal "now". Because light
takes four years to reach Earth from Proxima b, the closest star to
the sun, what I'm doing right now is four years in your future from
the moment you hear my voice, and your right "now" happened
four years ago for me. If we were to hold a conversation, what I
say and your reply back to me would take eight years. There is
an extended present that is neither past nor future, and it's in that
elsewhere that I make my home.

o

My longing telescopes. My flat becomes an infinite spaceport, one
continual lift-off fever dream. Every port is less of a place to move
through and more a state to slip into. Hello and welcome to the
endless country of always leaving your heart behind.

o

Whatever I am doing now is still four years away for you. We are
the slowest-moving storm, a study in otherworldly patience and
longitudinal data. Space is expanding faster and faster, and that is
no comfort either.

o

The fundamental asymmetry between a moment on Proxima b and the concept of a present here and now on Earth is a stress fracture broken over and over again. *Home / here / there / you / me / past / future / present / now* is a series of dislocations, and dislocations are never temporary. I fall out of love with now.

○

What it is like to love someone in outer space: Have you seen the video of an astronaut wringing out a wet towel? All that water squeezed out with nowhere to fall.

○

Say one day I finally land back on Earth and walk straight into your arms, wrung out with relief. Later that evening, we look through a telescope together and spot me on Proxima b, light years in the past, waving back at us. It is a feat of timing and engineering ingenuity and sweet-talking my way into borrowing office equipment for one night. Forgive me, this is just a thought experiment. Say, for a moment, I exist at two points, one a solid line of heat at your side and another, a wink of light in the sky already racing back to you. This is the only now I am grateful for.

○

The physics of spacetime doesn't care what our urgent human questions are. *Are you on your way home? I miss your voice; can you speak now? Have you eaten yet?* I wait eight lousy years for an answer. My skin hunger could fill a galaxy.

Homecoming

after Hala Alyan

In this version, you never leave Malaysia, never sell your house to your brother despite your father's boh tua boh suay comments. And why would you. You love that house on the lorong between jungle and the Guan Yin temple.

In this version, you leave Malaysia and America opens to you like an animal trap. Everywhere you go children chew their arms off to escape home at 18. Your new country loves freedom so much it's killing itself.

In this version you never leave Malaysia and your daughters grow up willful and wild as yam leaves. You love them the way the rainforest does: without abandon, drinking in the rainy season, rooting in the dry.

And if you had known differently?

You haven't yet told your daughter the saddest family secret she will one day have to know. It's hovering: a fist waiting to knock. Not yet. Not yet. Though she's asking, she's not ready yet.

Nightly, you rosary American synonyms for success learned the hard way: suburb – 10 year visa – promotion – carpool – mortgage – parent teacher conference – nuclear family – assimilation

You made your flight home. Your brother is dying, but you made your flight home. You thank every god that his wife doesn't baptise him on his deathbed, though she argues Christian funerals are less work than Chinese ones.

If having considered all the options, you decide on this one, know that:

Guan Yin has her hands full with you. Goddess of Compassion is pulling double shifts making sure the only thing that runs in this family are a tiger nose and a stubborn streak, wide as the Sarawak River.

Everywhere you go, you are already there. All your brothers are in the Arrivals hall, sweating through their t-shirts and cantankerously alive. They're waiting for you to gather up your bags.

In your beloved row house near the temple you almost married in, Cho Cho is telling you family secrets you never knew. The home you never stop leaving is wondering when you'll return. It is ready to devastate you all over again.

Homecoming is the last, hardest thing you'll ask yourself to do.

Malaysiana

a praise poem

Early morning blessing of
hawkers slinging noodles,
every face a sun through
clouds of starchy steam.
Reservoir Park at dawn. Clouds behind
Fort Margherita, a small sugared cake
on the riverbank. Golden state building
peaked like a 1950s cone bra.
Everyday things. Motorbikes gut gut guttering.
Out of season things.
Spiky knuckleduster
of durian. The suddenness
of sunrise on the equator,
you turn away for a second and *bam,*
it's filling the whole room.
Love, there's no such thing
as empty space in 100% humidity.
Daytime radio, Cantopopsicle melting
from an open car window.
Yellow-spined Nancy Drew
books handed down. Wet kitchens.
Wet market with their own gravity,
exoplanet of ice and fish
and tumble of fruit. Hibiscus tea.
Cats insistent at the back gate.
Geometric delight of layer kueh.
Papayas. Dipper baths, twice daily.
Five-foot way between a shop and the street
where someone is cutting
their neighbour's hair.
A whole street of
old-fashioned goldsmiths.

War hangover: talking about eating
when we're not finished with this meal.
Boiled peanuts. Chinese opera.
Friends' houses where we don't call ahead
but they know we're coming
anyway. Slow river sashay.
Wet laundry, like diligent flowers,
following the morning sun.
Marble-topped kopitiam tables.
Streets where you recognise everyone
and call out to each other,
how's your mother,
I saw your cousin the other day
playing badminton,
when are we going for liu cha.
Streets you can navigate
with your eyes closed.
Kumquat tree we watered for months
not knowing it was plastic.
Sally the adopted street mutt
and her benevolent gaze.
You're a tiny saint, Sally,
you're going straight to dog heaven.
Chinese moms don't say I love you,
they cut fruit for dessert, press
gold earrings into your palm,
buy 30 kilos of ginger
and cook all your post-partum
confinement meals for a month,
no questions asked.
Hand-washing our clothes
every morning makes us glad
to be in our skin.

Glitch honorifics

Cho Cho 祖祖 (great-grandmother)
Depending on your age and generation, she was Cho Cho or Poh Cho, degrees of veneration. In my mind she is deftly dealing cards under the dragon ceiling light. She is my grandmother in every way that counts, thought family secrets would tell you something different.

family history doesn't account my grandfather that was adopted the woman who would rise to me my great grandmother, not he uncle that was given away, e cousin-sisters cousin-brothers that ate at the table.

Ah Ma 阿嬤 (grandmother)
A line of mothers called by another name. When Ong Bee Leng married, there was already another relative with her name so she took a new one. She taught herself how to sew by unpicking seams of shirts. I think about the quiet, industrious buzz of her hands, another thread unspooled, line of us.

Lack of language is a longing. Hokkien is a fractal. Knowing only smatterings of traditional and simplified Chinese means seeing double, catching an half-formed ghost at the corner of your eye, four final strokes in the character for mother 媽 flattening into 妈 a maternal bloodline of four points – my great-grandmother, my grandmother, my mother and me – extending infinitely in two directions, past and future –

Everyday that you plant something and it survives is a triumph. Jungle knowledge. I count myself lucky in so many ways. Rojak girls, rojak dialect. When I travel back home, I'm already there.

On any given Sunday, I am the oldest kid in Chinese School. I can't shake the guilt that my closeness to Chinese is through the prism of mainland culture, a standardised Beijing accent, simplified strokes I still struggle to remember. This sterile Chinese is so far from Malaysia, it takes place in an elsewhere.

Drawing a family tree without Hokkien is like looking down a corridor of mirror doors. The leftover neon hum, cacophony of street signs in a night market, three unknowable dimensions flattened onto a single page –

Ah Ma 阿媽 (mother)
Assimilating as a small Chinese woman in America is difficult enough. You pack your mixed kids off to Chinese Sunday school and are chided by your sisters-in-law for not teaching them Hokkien. What for, la? To add another dimension of Malaysian-ness is a complication, amplifying otherness.

Ah Ee 阿姨 (cousin-sister)
Before we finish eating her kachama, we're already dreaming of the next meal. *Delicious* is one of the first Hokkien phrases I learn. *Busybody* is another.

Wa 我 (me)
If the line between my Ah Kong and Cho Cho is broken then we are occurring all at once, everyone before my time I didn't know and do now, existing at the same glitch point. We are occurring with rainy season predictability. Coming back to Malaysia feels like stepping into another self that exists in parallel.

Dream opera in Kuching

My 二舅 and 七舅 are in the kitchen. 二舅 is using an electric fly swatter as a conductor's baton to the intermezzo of chichaks and ancient ceiling fan and torrential rain. Live razor clams, pulsing in their long shells, wait to be steamed. 七舅 is hamming it up for the crowd. There's good whisky and a glass for everyone. He tells the story of how he drove his friend's expensive Jeep to the beach and got it stuck in water. Somewhere in the salt shallows, a rusting memory of teenaged recklessness. The aria of his arms move so fluidly at the punchline. I know this is a dream. It is a dream because I walk up to my 三舅 who is peeling an orange on the porch. I never knew him but here he is. Though in this dream I speak perfect Sarawak Hokkien, I don't need to. Even the pith is sweet.

Yellow

1.

黃 means yellow, means honey dragonfruit,
        custard apple, salted durian, a wet star cut true.
And your name became my name: untameable forsythia,
        a ribbon twining between us. Let's play a name game
of cat's cradle from Wee to Ooi and Uy and Ng.
        Blame the British and Dutch clerks sweating
through their regulation shirts in some upriver Borneo outpost,
        whose ears couldn't tell the difference.

2.

Your skin
the leather of papaya

left too long on the branch,
single persimmon bulb.

Let's call you halogen fruit
that burned brightest.

Let's call you the girl
that made it out of there.

3.

Who needs jewels when you have
yellow that is ancient and imperial
        that is banana cream paint
        that is the end of a purpling bruise
        that is the centre of the world
        that is oo ooh I am
        up to my neck in yellow
        that is joy, sure –

4.

A square of sunflowers
soaked in sugar syrup,
the perfect colonial-style house
we ached for, one beautiful
as a chiffon cake with
PTA mothers with perfect hair
who made sandwiches filled
with grape jam not beansprouts,
not growing French beans
in recycled milk gallons
by a chain link fence, not
sunning bedsheets in the yard –
what stupid sick roil of shame.
        Yellow that is joy, sure, but history too.
        Courage first.

5.

Whatever you do, don't burn out, she says in the garden
        under the yellow rambutan tree, where we eat
mother of pearl sweetness by the prickly handful.
        Moving is mourning. We are only together a short while,
she remarks, just travellers on the same path.
        My mother is sulphur fruit, sharp and bright
as lightning in a dry season, a whole wildfire blowing hard out ahead,
        clearing the way. Next to her, we are small hot stars
wheeling around fixed points. Sayang, love scorches
        clean through you. May it never go out.
May you warm your body by it. May it be furious and shining,
        backfire to any blaze barreling your way,
only a hot ache left in its place.

To become a dragon, first wear its skin

When she married, my mother wore a cheongsam
of red silk bright as a bolt of dragonfire. Her mother
tipped her from the bath and poured her into it, all
brimstone brilliance and the hottest part of the flame.
The tailoring perfect, each button knotted and curled
like a dragon's whiskers, and she liked that it was a touch
demure but slitted high enough on the thigh to turn heads.
The cool material felt like slipping out at night
to lie on your back in the sea, or the drawn-out pleasure
of a cigarette after sex, sheets pooled in the sticky heat.
Shoes, of course, buckled dragonskin. Imagine a bride,
knowing she could swallow any man whole. And later,
imagine a newlywed, packing a bag for his things
(coarse denim jacket stinking of hay and Oreo nicotine smell),
and finding the cheongsam at the back of the wardrobe,
pressed and forgotten. She cards her fingers through
whispering tissue, remembers the dress clinging like smoke.
Imagine memory as a whetstone. She sharpens herself on it.

There is no specific word in English for

father's younger brother's wife the way
there is a Hokkien honorific for exactly
this kinship : aunt (inadequate) : Ah Lian (shocking :
what self-respecting niece would dare
say her first name like that & who did
we think we were, American?) : no mother tongue
to call upon to gauge closeness and distance,
one tongue for seeing lightning
and another for counting thunder,
no word in English for the common local knowledge
that rain always stops for temple processions
like this one twining through town : rollicking
dragons chasing suns, neon lions chasing
dragons, Guan Yin girls bowing deeply
to a shophouse altar and boys hightailing
it out of there with a dragonfruit plucked
from the offering table : processions
gumming up traffic in open defiance
of the wet season : no word in English
for the name of the Tua Pek Kong temple deity
we were honouring with our attention,
all that halting shame slowly cranking through my body,
winched open like a stuck car window :
long held-off rain, waiting for small gods to pass through.

30 things Sarawakians know

after Michael Sorkin

1. Rain density by season.

2. The many uses of rozelle syrup.

3. The remediation capacity of mangroves.

4. Difference between primary and secondary forest, according to elevation.

5. Enough Malay, for official purposes.

6. Enough Teochew, for bartering purposes.

7. Enough Hakka, for gossip.

8. No matter what time your flight arrives, no matter the late hour, there will be someone to meet you and ask if you've eaten yet, who says *of course the night market is still open, we'll order one of everything.*

9. The difficulty of returning.

10. Plum salt with fresh cut fruit.

11. Burial practices and proper upkeep of ancestral graves, even if your children are Christian.

12. Cooling properties of sleeping on bamboo mats.

13. Distinguishing between the jingles of the morning vegetable truck and evening bread van.

14. To never cook sambal belachan without a wet kitchen, or if you must fry it indoors, cut 20 limau kasturi into a pot of boiling water & turn on every fan & open all your windows as wide as they'll go & resign yourself to smelling it on your clothes for days.

15. Migratory patterns of children.

16. Counteracting durian by drinking saltwater from its shell.

17. Who to call when you accidentally drive your car into a ditch, in the pouring rain, nine miles out of town.

18. Who will show up despite everything.

19. The way prayer carries over water.

20. An appreciation for quality kachama.

21. Particularly kachama from that restaurant by Hong Leong bank, near the popiah place on Ban Hock Road.

22. The popiah place on Ban Hock Road.

23. The predictability of storms.

24. How to massage bitterness out of mani cai with salt.

25. Sarsaparilla ice cream float.

26. The distance between kampungs as measured in cigarette breaks.

27. That travellers palm plants hold water, in a pinch.

28. Pointing with your lips.

29. Whose house you can walk straight into without invitation.

30. The density of family in the surrounding area needed for a spontaneous potluck.

Feast Day

One of these days I'll make
every single recipe
from the beautiful cookbooks
you've gifted me all these years
and which I keep with good intentions.
I'll invite everyone round,
they'll sit on the floor, lean against
sofa legs, balancing plates
on their laps and asking for seconds.
It'll be an all-day open house:
us in the kitchen, hip-checking
drawers closed, topping up drinks,
singing out to the crowd
in the living room, me sending you
to the cornershop for a single lemon.
I announce the arrival
of the next course like guests
at a fancy ball: mountains of
buttery pilaf; gunpowder potatoes;
Nalli Nihari lamb falling off the bone;
serrated sugar crust of caramelised peaches;
and for dessert, the crowning glory,
cherry pie still bubbling from the oven
and its magnificent golden coat of pastry.
Years later, we'll still remember it,
how the house had never been so full.

Social distancing

after Charles Simic

It was the epoch of transmutation. Some evenings the neighbours turned into jaguars and dragged their dinner up into the trees. You could touch anything you wanted and watch it change. A bench became a hammerhead shark. Confetti became slices of wet ham. A postbox: a baby grand piano. Where Town Hall once stood, now was a giant baklava oozing honey. Someone turned their arm into long tentacles of squirming fingers and went trawling, terrorising the streets by grasping everything in reach. We were afraid to venture out of our homes.

Everything became a record of what we touched, or hadn't – where our hands lingered, or didn't – how much distance we could afford to put between ourselves and others – what it cost us, what it didn't.

Eurydice video calls her lover in lockdown

Seeing each other like this doesn't count,
we aren't breaking any divine rules.
Look all you want. Everyone here
is on a long distance call, speaking to someone
already slipping out of memory.
O. is showing me a tiny succulent
he thought was a goner. His hands
are gorgeous, a suggestion of palm on screen holding
a red flower on a leggy plant surging towards light.
One etiolated thing looking at another.
I want you to hang up, defy the gods,
touch me. I'm downright ravenous.
You think it's bad up there; baby, ghosts just pass
through each other, yearning yearning yearning.
I want you to carry me out of here
bridal-style or fireman-lift, I'm not picky.
I'm waiting for the all-clear, someone to shout
olly olly oxen free, won't you come out Eurydice.
I'm not sure what I want more: certainty,
or to finally set down this longing.

~

BLOOM

~

[it begins]

after Nuar Alsadir

Hemingway would record every detail of an event – say a bomb – and then take out the event and leave only the reverberations. That is as good a description of jellyfish as you'll get. Watch out for my rippling legs, a fry of glass eels drifting up the shore. We bloom like nuclear hydrangea. In certain light conditions, you won't notice until it's too late, our iridescent bells marking out the radius of our poisonous reach. Boom. This year we are startlingly large and daring.

~

[the world's longest creature is observed]

For scientists, coming across the never-before-seen
siphonophore off the cost of Western Australia

would have been like finding a UFO in the backyard.
Like a six year old hearing radio signals

from a far-off, undiscovered galaxy
through a tin can telephone.

People and jellyfish are AM and FM radio waves,
passing each other in the same space,

unaware of each other's existence.
But back to me. Aren't I something?

I'm an unwound chandelier,
a 150-foot-long coil of cilia,

made up of a million gelatinous foxgloves.
Calling me unearthly shows how small your world is.

~

[trip]

When stung by box jellyfish, you start hallucinating immediately. Our venom salt-washes the world in neon. The ground tilts up, a dizzying escalator. Watch out for the sour swoop in your stomach, like waiting in an infinite departure lounge when your flight has already left for home. Distance accordions in the virtual airport. Everywhere you turn is an exit point, a plane peeling up into darkness. The return leg is always dicey.

~

[survival of the fittest]

The stomach contents of the beached sperm whale:
   glow sticks, squid mandibles, plastic carrier bags, punctured balloons,
   3 metres of eyelet lace, a freshwater pearl necklace.

Our bloom is a new species entirely, evolved from:
   glow sticks, squid mandibles, plastic carrier bags, punctured balloons,
   3 metres of eyelet lace, a freshwater pearl necklace.

In the harbour, in full view of local and national media we have assembled
for the occasion, we arrange ourselves into the shape of an eye and wink.

~

[domestication]

We were bred in salad bowls
and the indignity of paddling pools.

One local entrepreneur,
facing the prospect of a quiet summer

with beaches closed and fishing decimated,
started breeding us as pets.

Every day he squirted pink krill
from a water pistol into our waiting mouths.

$5 for a teacup moon jelly / 3 for $12.
Our friends, Goldfish Against Goldfish

In Plastic Baggies At Fairgrounds,
swam in solidarity from a distance.

~

[spineless menace]

Only the best and brightest jellyfish are allowed in our waters, the government announced at the launch of the joint Jellyfish Immigration and Economic Strategy. Without heart, brains or blood, the Home Secretary said, these invasive species do not contribute as much to the system as they take out. Exemptions will be granted in exceptional circumstances: jellyfish willing to be pulped for agricultural fertiliser to help farmers feed the nation can fast-track their visa applications. NO RECOURSE TO PUBLIC FUNDS will be stamped in squid ink on every tentacle.

~

[threat level]

You have very limited ways of

experiencing and seeing us alive.

When you think jellyfish you think

stingy, gooey, scary, gross.

You only know what threatens you.

You brace for pain like the plane is going down.

We survive oil spills, acidic oceans,

nuclear tests, fertiliser run-offs.

In such conditions, life seems improbable.

In some blooms, there is more jelly than water.

You wonder how we keep breathing.

You are very benevolent to let us live.

At the end of the world there will be cockroaches.

Cockroaches, and jellyfish.

~

[cassandra]

I hope you never have to know the lumens
    of a panicked jellyfish

I hope you never turn your body into a beacon
    to light signal fires along an ocean ridge

I hope your eyes never tire from
    keeping everything in your sight

I hope you never have to
    explain away your existence

I hope you never feel the need to snip a hole
    out of the present and slip through

I hope you never have a migraine
    open at your temples like an aurora

I hope you never have bioluminescent nightmares
    the colour of this country's threat level

I hope you never have to bear witness to
    what one jellyfish can do to another

I hope you never feel unsafe in your own body
    of water

                night is dark enough as it is

~

[zero gravity]

To absolutely no one's surprise, jellyfish born in space don't do
so hot back on Earth / we pulsed dully / couldn't tell up from
down / couldn't push the soft suck of our bodies through water
/ preferred artificial seawater and the spaceshuttle bilge we were
raised in / swam in slow distressed circles / whorl of inner ear
disrupted / wet tangle of nerve cells / a severed satellite link / we
cycled through every frequency in vain / vertigo so distressing
it was like looking at Vantablack / hot shivery wrongness of
looking over a cliff / an internal alarm warning you could tumble
out of space if we got too close / NASA researchers would later
report that their experimental jellyfish developed vertigo / like
it was just rollercoaster dizziness / silliness of space mountain
+ dehydration + mild sunstroke + funnel cake sugar high / my
vertigo is finding / my house gone / the sea drained / no record of
it on any map / and all my children grown and left / I'm the loose
elastic of old underwear / clinging to a soft body to slow my slide
/ at least Cassini was given the dignity of crashing

~

Poet's note: In 1991, NASA sent thousands of jellyfish polyps into outer
space on the space shuttle Columbia to study how creatures grow in
microgravity. At one point, there were 60,000 moon jellyfish in orbit. These
jellyfish later developed vertigo and abnormal swimming patterns. The
findings were troubling, with implications for long-term space travel and
the prospects of human babies born in outer space.

[moon jellies escape]

We launched ourselves out of the airlock,
plotted an uprising, bolts of iridescent
moon jellies lunging into space like blue greyhounds,
daring and unstoppable, hollering in light.
We who were bred in zero gravity and artificial seawater
dreamed of this moonshot escape,
bloom loosened, troop of moonlets marvelling
at the instinctive pull towards any lunar body
we could call our own. So many of us
that a blue nebula was visible on Earth at high noon.
For one moment people stopped, the whole world
tipping its head back in wonder.
Blue is such an inadequate word
for what happened that day: ultramarine,
lapis lazuli neon, holy Sassoferrato blue, wet voltage blue,
heavens the colour of the hottest part of the flame.
Houston, there are 60,000 moonmoons
in the sky right now, and each one your doing.
Maybe that's why the moon is moving away
from the Earth a few centimetres every year
– to make room for your hubris.

The collective noun for us is an astonishment.

~ ○ ~

Sonnet with lighthouses

The first lighthouse is you.

The second lighthouse is you, age 12, turned around beneath a wave.

The third lighthouse is a hyperbaric chamber you clamber into when you dive too deep and rise too fast, an oil-dark depth that's child's play for trained divers but you, girl, you clawed yourself up –

The fourth lighthouse tunes into the shipping song over sea static: rain later, good, occasionally poor.

The fifth lighthouse says over and over, I love you I love you I love you you you you there.

Every wall in the sixth lighthouse is load-bearing.

The seventh lighthouse is a scattergram of light that indicates the strength and direction between two variables: ship and safe harbour, moon and tide, shore and vagaries of current, each of us to each other, our future selves to our past selves, every dear friend placed at strategic vantage points in our life.

Just seeing the eighth lighthouse strengthens your circuitry, blood zinging around your bones in delight.

The ninth lighthouse has *worse things happen at sea* cheerfully cross-stitched on a pillow it bought drunk off Etsy.

The tenth lighthouse sometimes just wants to be a lifeboat or a ladder or an oxygen mask, dropped down in case of emergencies and not always looking out for other people when they can't help themselves.

The eleventh lighthouse's favourite piece of furniture is the walnut drop-leaf table that opens so everyone can fit around it.

The twelfth lighthouse makes you feel like stepping out of time.

The thirteenth lighthouse comforts you with Fermat's mathematical proof which shows that light knows where it's going, that it takes the shortest possible route, even through water and gale forces.

The fourteenth lighthouse hollers MARCO.

                           POLO, everyone you love shouts back.

The Home Office

after Caroline Bird

The motivational poster that says, *I want YOU*
to make this environment more hostile.
The hallway that elongates like an infernal scream.
The doors that open onto the room you just exited.
The stairwell that spits you out in another country.
The anonymous senior source that leaks the story
to the Sunday papers. Who is in the archives
wading knee-deep through documents
that don't officially exist. Who takes a long drag
of a cigarette and says, "Landing cards?
Why, I haven't heard that phrase in years."
Who clicks a lighter under the sprinklers.
Who switches on industrial-grade shredders.
Who dumps passports by the box
into a bathtub of lime-green acid.
Whose daily stroll along the Thames
makes fish swim backwards and belly up.
Who loves the smell of closed borders in the morning.
Who chants "best and brightest" in the mirror three times
with the lights off. Who is replacing all your framed photos with
glacé eel eyes that scuttle over the floorboards at night.
Who doesn't see the irony in the phrase "Leave to Remain".
Who is flipping a coin to decide your settled status:
heads we win, tails you lose. Who feeds your housekeys
to a pet alligator to see how bad you want them back.
Who paints miniature houses like a Christmas village
and displays them in a locked trophy case: mementos of
all the homes we loved and lived in, or might have lived in,
or dreamt of, or passed through, or were evicted from,

or ran towards or put up with. Who cheerfully
mails you postcards that say "Wish you were here!"
after deporting you. Who scooped out
a whale like a rotting pumpkin and stuffed it
with infrared trackers and launched it back into the Channel
to alert them to foreign bodies in the sea.
Who thinks of all this dark, dark water.
Whose dreams are choked with pond scum.
Who believes that someone, somewhere, somehow,
isn't where they should be, and it's up to
the Home Office to do something about it.
No doubt there's a boat clawing its way to shore
right at this very moment. You see,
nobody necessarily stays anywhere forever.

Leave

Home is a weapon that you lift
to your shoulder, a cool promise
against your skin. Home is a
series of possibilities.

There are eviction notices in
graffiti: get out. There is a brick
through the window, there is
a man in every room in your house.

You'll be okay from here.
It's not a question.
You walk around in such thin skin
under a sky blue and headstrong.

There are paper tigers pacing the rafters.
You fear the front yard has turned
to quicksand. Someone's been planting
little bombs under the magnolia tree.

All your limbs are so heavy,
you have been running for days.
You have carried everyone you love,
and for so long, and over such distances.

Home is the wrongness of a muzzle
at the door, the heart's dark chamber,
it's climbing into the black mouth
of a lion and trusting him not to snap.

Loving v. Virginia

Stand with me in the full-fat American sunshine in all the places where we love each other: across state lines, courthouse steps, porch swings with seventeen fireflies for lamps, nothing forgotten or lost. Let me tell you about the orderly pursuit of happiness, summer undeterred, sucking stars on your shoulder, police vans swaying like sleep-warm bodies in the dark, the road always turning home. My beautiful boy, don't be afraid of loving. Are you getting all this down? There can be no question. There can be no doubt of liberty. Let me tell you who to love – no. Let me tell you how – yes: earth smelling of good mint, a skinny beanpole of a guy, the long lick of your back a furnace, sweet sweat pooling behind knees. The officer's expression like a door in the face and better a door than a fist, better a fist than your body bowing in the stand, good suit creasing, and better a body in the stand than beaten. This is what I mean when I say unruly, you stubborn thing. Look at us, improper. Look at us, indecent. Look at us, incandescent and loving.

If given a choice, my boyfriend wants to be immortal

The opposite of death isn't being a god, it's not caring about change. No,
I want the full terror and joy of life hurtling through me. Broken arm,
pink cast. Jelly legs when the elevator loses power. I want to swim out
into deep waters like I'm striking out, swinging for the fences. I want to
grow old with you. I want to see your hair go salt and pepper, I want
to chide you about sunscreen until we are as are wrinkled as old plums
or the chestnut mushrooms I rescue from the back of the crisper. I want
all the terror, all the sweetness, I want the urgency zinging through
me. I want to be a small meteor shower, no great comet so dazzling as to
garner a god's attention, just bright enough to make you smile. I want to
drive through fields crammed with sunflowers in a French convertible
and red lipstick and feel sexy and sun-warmed and so turned on by
your right hand on the gearshift I'm a swarm of summer cicadas,
crawling out of my skin. I even want the email from my dad writing
to say he is free from the cancer we didn't know he had in the first
place. I want to know it won't last, but we chose to be in it, fully in it,
canonballing until the water closes up above our heads. What's this to a
lifetime of lives. What's infinite time to a multiplicity of universes. How
could you ever think eons would compare to this.

Scheherezade in the care home

1.

& do you remember how all the king's horses bowed before him —

& do you remember cool sheets like muslin rain —

& do you remember running for the train in the night —

& do you remember the soldier's hand at your throat —

& do you remember holding yourself open, a little door
into the dark —

& do you remember when we came to this country we —

& do you remember how we made ambrosia salad
with mandarin pieces in syrup, Cool Whip, pecans,
tiny marshmallows softer than a kitten's paw —

& do you remember the sword hanging over my head —

& do you remember —

& when are we going home?

2.

Not too long ago you are in a room where she is just a tiny slip of a thing in her zinnia print overcoat, already faded, hiding small hands tucked into the knit blanket. You bring her a silk scarf, peeled pomegranate, photos of her grandchildren at birthday parties, 4th of July parades, prom. Oh, she says, there you are, her smile bright and clean. Her gaze a whole dark field. On the old TV set is a nature documentary about how wolves change rivers, how fragile equilibrium is, how we chase it like mouths in the dark. Okay, Sharon, the nurse says not unkindly, and sets down a cup of green jello.

3.

Dear world, each night you turn me over
and it is like picking up your child

after a long absence, a hasty deportation, say,
or exile, and being surprised by the sudden weight,

the warmth in your arms. Dear world,
winter is my favourite season

because dawn lasts all day. Now talk radio fills
the room like a lung, silence like pneumothorax

and I am at the centre of it, a collapsed star,
only old light left behind to reach you.

You are two pockets of loose change,
a bus ticket bought by a kind stranger, a fake ID,

a duffle bag of clothes, sweet butter, thumb of ginger.
Dear world, as an immigrant I fell in love with you,

held you more fiercely because this home
was not mine, loved the way a wild thing

thrashes moments before the hunter's
fingers dig into its scruff.

Darling, when your neck is on the line
every morning is a chance to kiss someone whole again.

4.

In the room is a woman that is a thousand and one
beautiful things: a penny that keeps turning up,
a slice of melon like December sunshine.
She always looks surprised to see us. Her hair
is oiled and pinned, like we caught her just
as she was heading out to meet someone important,
a king or a kingmaker. I am learning-family-secrets years old.
I am convinced angels are grandmothers who forgot
all the unkind things we've done. Ours is a minor history,
easily overlooked. What's a liar to a storyteller.
Piety: old strong magic of Sunday visits to the care home,
the swift, gripping current of my mother's gaze
in the rearview mirror, pinioning me, all but daring
me to complain. Why are we here, if not for each other.

5.

The hour in which I love you
               smells of
       citrus and
                    candied peel.
     Forgive an old woman
her enamel heart.
               I want to walk through a boulevard
     of orange trees
          in a white sundress
with an outrageous sunhat.
          I've always looked great in hats   still do.
     You've been gone too long.
                Is it time for the therapy animals yet?
     When I was little,
        we climbed into
          the pink tulle
of the cherry trees and stayed there until dinner.
     I would like that sundress now
        impractical   as it is.

Abridged dictionary for water babies

FIR   Pine honey is salt sap, bark treacle, sharper and greener and colder than anything collected from inland hives.

FISH   When I said I hated seafood my mother said like hell and brought me to the market until I learned to love it, even at 3 a.m., learned to love the tuna fillets like huge horse hearts kicking over, strawberry grouper, Halibut Joey's hollered hello, those little chits and old-fashioned scales, loved the watchful hum of warehouse lights, this bright knot of sea at the dark margin of a sleeping city.

MOON   Jellied fish eye, prized delicacy, unblinking above dark cliffs.

SALT   -lined -circle -crust -glaze -water

SELKIE   I am forever half-one thing, half-something else. If I chanted *lissom* like a spell enough times I could wriggle into it like a nylon dress. I am wringing out my skin until the whole house smells like engine oil, seaweed, a promise: tomorrow.

VENUS   Lisa stepped out in a gold sequin swimsuit like a rockstar. Where do you even get a suit like that. She even brought an inflatable scallop shell. Everything matched, her sun-lightened curls, glitter nails, glitter sunglasses. We sat around like lesser nereids in our plain wetsuits. It was like looking straight into the sun and she goddamn knew it.

WATER   Even as we were in it we longed to be in it, forever sculling between shallows and the ocean floor dropping away into dark blue, sea-greedy, our weird tan lines, our Vaselined armpits. All summer long, the small boat of my heart takes on water.

Judith & the head of Holofernes

I am 100% Alka Seltzer and I burn the whole way down. Every woman is stealing into the general's hut – sister, saviour, slut – severing ties with our better angels. Sirens are leading men to their deaths. Every day is a state of emergency. Every woman I know is leading herself out of the dark, unfurling the cage of her ribs and clambering up like a fire escape. Our bodies were built for this. Two hands sending up flares, bracing for impact, hacking a hole in the roof, it's getting your own way, no, it's knowing how to get out of your own way. Indelible in the hippocampus is knowing that cruelty is the point, a weaponised disbelief. I am looking you dead in the eye. Freedom is what dreams do for the waking. One day, I'll escape on a plane of my own making, twin engines gunning.

The impossible physiology of the free diver

By the time this poem ends, the hummingbird
you're thinking of might be dead,
a hard-boiled ruby sweet in the grass.

○

A billion heartbeats in a lifetime
is all we get; the slower your pulse
the longer you live.
Did you know the left lung shares
space with the heart, that
a free diver's lungs compresses
to the size of two apples?

○

At Allie's tenth birthday party,
among bright bathing suits,
pink lemonade blooming
where it spilled in the shallow end,
the sun a hot stone fruit,
I crossed my legs and sank
down in the community pool
to see how long I could hold my breath,
stop time, and just for a moment
I was a little god on the floor
of the world looking up.

○

There is a religious flyer trapped
in the screen door that reassures:
You have so much more living to do.
A moment, please,
for the heart yammering away,
the heart standing on the porch,
the heart measuring breaths like levelling sugar
for a batter, the heart saying
why don't you come in from the cold.

And how later a mother wakes
in the night to her two year old's cough,
carrying him in her arms
to the steamed-up bathroom,
scrabbling for Vicks,
panic as big as the sea, its inevitable gravity,
poor lungs the size of a crabapple,
her hummingbird heart in her mouth.
She rucks up his shirt, touches his small back.
How the heart murmurs
breathe, baby, breathe.

Moon goddess ghazal

A man walks into the forest for the last time.
The air smells portentous, like wet dog. He moons

over me, dumbstruck. In paintings, I'm always
startled & doe-shy, a naked slip of crescent moon.

Now dryads are cat-calling in the trees. No, they're whistling
his deerhounds to their dinner. Under this petty moon

honey burns. Mint curdles. I'm one long nettle scream.
Sorry for the abject chaos, I needed the attention. Full moon

craziness is licking lightning or unzipping
your sternum to find a black bear baying. Good moon

goddesses aren't meant to wear lycra shorts under dresses,
shed antlers, talk back to the dark. I'm moonlighting

under one of my lesser names these days – Cynthia,
what quickens in the night? Blood. Hunger. A hunter's moon.

Birds flimed in slow motion from a moving car

make the world look like it's come to a halt.

The whole scene a lenticular picture
    like a 90s bookmark
        moving slightly as the ground tilted

a few degrees left then right,
    the flock suspended in looping circles
        above our red station wagon.

According to contemporary physics,
    time as we know it doesn't really exist,
        things just change in relation to each other.

Here, we used to visit
    Minnesota family every summer break
        and Christmas until we stopped,

got busy, I guess, the way life does.
    Cousins grow apart. Right now, the sky
        never looked so close –

if we had the right shoes & plenty runway
    & jumped high enough we could skim
        that blue with our hands.

Shell game

1.

A friend once asked: in difficult moments,
do you close yourself or open to it? I wish
I could measure the impact of that question.

2.

Clearing out grandma's farm, my family found
flood-soaked boxes of home videos
and went to Walmart and turned them into DVDs.
My aunt fusses over us, brings in trays
of her wild rice soup we always beg her
to make. It's so thick we practically have to slice it up.

3.

Look, she says, there's your dad in his Christening outfit.
That's the one your cousins wore too, if you can believe it.
There's your dad and your uncle horsing around in their cowboy outfits.
Who's birthday party was that? The tractor, the good farm dog,
the red barn. Now it's Christmas. The ——— cousins must have stayed with us
that year. Did your dad ever tell you about his 4H prize-winning sheep.
No, your aunts weren't born yet. Look, she says,
wasn't that you, there at the edge of the frame?

4.

Sometimes the timelines blur, merge a little so I can't remember to
which a particular moment belongs. It's a shell game of memories. I
can't remember if this is the reality where my parents married under
a moon arch, where Grandpa lived or died, where we forgot to stay
in touch, where we came back to —— every Christmas and decorated
sugar cookies and watched *Home Alone*, where we went to midnight
mass, where —— made a habit of scaring ——'s college boyfriends
silly, where for a few weeks —— backpacked through Europe and fell
in love out there. I can't remember if this is the timeline where ——
became an immigration lawyer or —— took the Fulbright scholarship.
Where Grandma always remembered to end the phone call with
remember you are loved even as she remembered nothing else. I can't
remember if all of us – my sister, my dad, his sister – ever sat this close,
if we ever talked about anything important at all. I can't remember but
it feels inevitable: us skipping through each quickening frame like we
knew what was coming and wouldn't change a thing.

5.

My aunt has an easy prayer
she uses like a kitchen stool
to reach the things she cannot see.

6.

The ordinary amazement of watching
my aging father watch himself on 60 year old
film, developed only through the sheer
luck of it being in a box that escaped flooding
that winter. The shaky camera carried by my long-dead
grandfather I never knew and whose name
now escapes me, this unseen hand reeling
us into existence. Afternoon light draping
us all in the den, and the chunks of pink
ham I chased around slivers of carrot
in the wild rice soup my aunt had
cooked that morning in anticipation
of our visit.

7.

A friend once asked: in difficult moments,
do you close yourself or open to it?
The same dream: one room full of doors,
wood and brass and beckoning greedily.
Sometimes the whole dream is just
waiting on the threshold until I wake up.

Persimmon abecedarian

Arriving with a skin-memory of sun, my mother
buys persimmons at the Turkish
corner shop. Imagine flying such
distances to be here, squeezed between own-brand cornflakes,
energy bars, long-life milk. Imagine not loving the audacity of this
fluorescent fruit, fistful of radiance, its neon sugar
gurgling out of its glossy peel. Every second generation is a
hagiography of mothers crossing seas for someone.
Imagine that, persimmons in the UK. Imagine
jostling towards cold weather and unfamiliar countries
knowing it's the opposite direction of every
loved thing left behind. I rinse, she slices. These
mellow suns as close as we'll get to eating solid honey. Chinese
New Year calls for sweet, round things. I add
oranges to the shopping list. This is my
personal definition of luminous, a
quiet moment in the kitchen, my mother chiding me
Remember to call home from time to time.
Saints have their haloes, my mother has a bowl of
twilight radiance she'll stand at the sink and eat
until the whole bag is gone, working
voraciously, fruit juice constellating my countertops, nothing
wasted, yes, sweet, yes, gobbled too fast.
Xylophone of stripped trees is tapping at the glass. A full
year is too long to go without seeing each other again. Winter is
zipping up the window, turning us in toward each other.

Lupins

It never occurred to me
to ask where purple honey

           comes from but it must
           be the lupins that stand

like tiny sentries
at parade attention,

           sticks of blue raspberry
           rock candy, azalea jazz,

early plums, stars jangling
like spurs or new pennies,

           grape soda, lapis prayer, pokeberry
           plaits, soft and woollen,

salt spray of violet so heady
it hurts to look straight at it.

           Such indigo light
           like windfall fruit

rioting up the hill
and down to the sea.

           Some days
           their purple spines

are the only things
holding me up.

Paddling at dusk, Winslow Homer, watercolor on paper (1892)

There's no word as lovely as canoe.
Scooping out loon birds, sound

like a hollowing out with two hands.
The lake is rough as a bolt of blue linen.

In this unlikely lapis light
you can't tell oar from silver otter,

man from the mountain
he's disappearing into,

can't tell thirst until
you reach open water.

Drokpa

"Longing, we say, because desire is full / of endless distances."
    – Robert Hass

In another life, my father
must have been a nomad.
He drinks butter tea,
knows his way around a saddle,
turns the living room into open rangeland.
There are horses at the door,
nudging their big noses into the hallway,
familiar to him as brothers.
Everywhere we turn they are
stamping down the carpet, swinging wide,
sweating hard, and right in the centre
of that heaving bunch of muscle,
dad pours out the door like wind,
loose bridle, easy seat, running like hell.
In Tibetan, drokpa means 'people of the solitudes',
as if solitude was open country
in which we learn early
to lean into the gale, to forage old ground.
He does not dwell long,
disappears for seasons at a time
and we came to realise the way he loves
is the way a horse makes a break for it,
steaming, impatient, expectant,
body corded tight. Horses like clouds
scudding across fields of grass, wild iris,
lashed canvas. He takes off, bad back and all.
His heart opens like a valley.

How to perfect a flip turn

The first thing to remember about flip turns
is that they are made blind. Don't look ahead

to the wall or to your legs. Trust that
for once your body will not fight itself,

trust that grace comes easy as breathing.
It's a delicious thrill, darting through water

& your whole self jonseing
with chlorine want & for once your limbs

perfectly long & lean & your body caught
in its own headlong momentum.

The moment before the turn is like
opening a window to unexpected birdsong

despite rain and the late hour. It is never
wanting for anything except the easy slip

of your body in its spandex skin.
You kick off wherever your feet land.

Voicemails from my mother

An old story, one you know:
Once a snake ate my cat so
my second brother killed it
dead and made snake ball
soup for the whole family.
Maybe next time our table
will be bigger. Next time,
a snake big enough to feed
the street. Remember, I taught
you which palms to drink from,
how to pinch thin moons of dough
around the filling. I am running
out of time to tell you everything.
I can't for the life of me remember
what I called to say. Don't be stupid,
no one died of homesickness.
What a waste a one-way ticket
would be. Sayang, I'm sorry if
I woke you up. Sayang, everything
here tastes different – fish fried
in black oil and Maggi Magic Sarap.
Missy brought her youngest daughter
to lunch today – you know Isabel,
the one at Yale – she reminded me
of you, or perhaps you are still that way.
I thought I'd spend a year here
but fruit trees take a year to yield anything.
I'm going out to the field today.
The light is doing something new
and it's time for planting.

Sayang, everything that's dead is just fertiliser.
All I need I can carry in my hands.
I liked me best when I chose to leave.
What I took with me, who I left,
there at the border,
squinting a little, raising a hand.

Notes

'30 Things Sarawakians Should Know' is after architect Michael Sorkin's '250 Things an Architect Should Know'. I came across it through the 99% Invisible podcast episode titled 'The Smell of Concrete After Rain'.

The last line of 'The Home Office', "Nobody necessarily stays anywhere forever", is a direct quote from then Home Secretary Theresa May in 2016. It was her response when asked in an interview about whether EU migrants would be allowed to stay in the UK.

'Loving v. Virginia' refers to Supreme Court case Loving v. the Commonwealth of Virginia, a landmark civil rights ruling in 1967 that struck down state laws banning interracial marriage in the United States.

'Moon jellies escape' mentions a 'moonmoon', which is a moon that orbits other moons, also known as a submoon or a subsatellite.

'Drokpa' is titled after a book written by my father, *Drokpa: Nomads of the Tibetan Plateau and Himalaya*.

Acknowledgements

Many thanks to the editors of the following publications in which some of these poems first appeared, sometimes in different forms:

Ambit, Poetry Birmingham Literary Journal, Under the Radar, harana poetry and *Butcher's Dog*. 'Yellow', 'Leave', 'The impossible physiology of the free diver', 'Drokpa', 'Lupins' and 'Scheherezade 1. and 2.' were published in *Primers: Volume Two,* also from Nine Arches Press. 'To become a dragon first wear its skin' won first prize in the in the Plough Poetry Competition 2018. 'Judith & the head of Holofernes' was commissioned by Writing West Midlands for National Poetry Day.

Thank you to editor and publisher Jane Commane, for believing in my writing all these years.

This collection wouldn't have been written without poetry friends and brilliant mentors: Jenna Clake, Romalyn Ante, Ron Villanueva, Khairani Barokka, Troy Cabida, Jonathan Davidson, Roy McFarlane and Emma Wright. My heartfelt gratitude to Stu Bartholomew, who read an early draft of this manuscript, for his generosity and unwavering encouragement. I'd also like to thank the Poetry School and Ann & Peter Samson, on whose courses many of these poems were initially written. Thank you Abby, Phoebe, Ananya, Alex S. and Jane P. – your friendship means the world.

All my love to my family – Mom, Dad, Ashley, as well as extended family in Malaysia and Minnesota – who are the beating heart of this book.

And thank you Rackesh, for everything, always.